Breakers of Barriers

Five Stunning Stories of People Demolishing Walls to Make History

Nury Vittachi

Illustrations by Step Cheung

Contents

STEP C.

THE UNLOVED TEENAGER AND THE GIANT CALCULATOR

ADA WAS A BAD GIRL. And no one was surprised. (As a teenager, she had run off with a man, causing a family scandal.) It was all because of her father, people said — he was famous for being an immoral person.

But the story of this particular teenage girl is worth remembering for several reasons.

First, have you heard of children who are born very rich in terms of money, but very poor in terms of love?

Well, that was Augusta Byron, known as Ada, who was born in the UK in 1815.

She was born into the middle of a furious argument between her parents, who were always fighting.

Her father was a brilliant man named Lord Byron, who was a wonderful writer but a dreadful husband and father. He treated his wife badly, and had lots of girlfriends, some of whom he also made pregnant.

A month after Ada was born, Lord Byron stormed out of the house, never to return.

Often people can survive without a father, since they at least have mothers — but in Ada's case, her mother was almost as bad as her father.

Her mother didn't care much for her own child, leaving her with her grandmother. The woman pretended to like occasionally spending time with "it" (that's what she called her child) so that if the marriage was examined in a divorce court, she could claim she'd been a good parent.

By the time Ada was 17, she was behaving badly, and ran off to elope with her tutor — but her family took her back and hushed up the scandal.

Then, when she was 18, her next tutor (a woman, this time) noticed she was good at mathematics and introduced her to a man named Charles Babbage, who was creating something very strange — a giant calculator.

Ada became his assistant.

He explained to her how his machine worked. She was very bright and understood it, and she wrote down the process of how the giant calculator worked. (He called it "the Difference Engine", because you pulled a lever and it instantly worked out the difference between two numbers.)

Well, if you recognize the name Charles Babbage, you will be able to guess the end of the story.

Charles Babbage is now in the history books as the inventor of the first computer — which was a mechanical device. (Much later, Alan Turing invented the electronic version of the computer.)

And Ada Lovelace (she became famous under the family name of the man she eventually married) became the world's first computer programmer.

The next time you use a computer, maybe look up and say a word of thanks to the girl, unloved by her father or her mother, who took the one skill she did have and made a difference to history with it.

THE SCIENTIST AND THE SECRET IN THE ANCIENT BOOK

A FATHER THINKING ABOUT a name for his newborn daughter read a line in a poem: "The deer make a you-you sound as they eat the wild hao plants."

The man, whose name was Tu, decided that he liked that sound, and named his bright daughter Youyou.

But as she grew up in the 1930s and 1940s, he felt that the political situation was unstable and trouble lay ahead.

He would soon be proved right. Little Youyou did well at her school in Ningbo, China, and went on to study pharmaceuticals and Chinese traditional medicine at university.

But then disaster struck. In the 1960s, a political movement in China called the Cultural Revolution put all scientists onto a blacklist.

Youyou and her husband, also a scientist, were sent to work on a farm, and their child sent to a nursery. Tu Youyou also expected to be shamed and banished.

Her family had been broken up and the future seemed dark.

But China's leader, Mao Zedong, had a secret. He needed at least a few scientists to keep working, because he wanted to find a cure for a killer disease, a type of malaria, which was killing soldiers.

He set up a top-secret department called Project 523. The number came from the date the operation started: May 23, 1967.

So Tu Youyou was commissioned to find a cure for an incurable strain of a deadly disease.

It seemed an impossible task. By that stage, scientists around the world had tested more than 240,000 compounds and none of them worked.

The global scientific community had failed.

Tu Youyou, who had come from a book-loving family, had an idea — instead of going to the lab, she went to the library (another thing that the ruling party did not approve of).

She read ancient texts which featured traditional wisdom.

The scientist found a 1,600-year-old recipe with a curious title: "Emergency Prescriptions to Keep up One's Sleeve". It called for the use of the extract of a Chinese herb called qinghao, or just hao for short.

But she recalled that they had boiled that plant to check its extract, and it had failed to make any difference.

Then, in a paragraph written in AD 340, she read that the essence of the hao plant should be extracted in cold water only.

She tried again with cold water — and this time it worked, killing the malaria parasite. She needed a human volunteer to take it, to prove that it was safe, and she chose herself.

Tu Youyou's medicine worked remarkably well, and has now saved countless lives around the world.

The Cultural Revolution came to an end, and she was reunited with her family.

Her achievement was celebrated worldwide when she was given the Nobel Prize.

But when she reflected on her life, she noticed something curious.

She picked up her father's book of poetry and noticed that his favorite line mentioned the sound that had given her her name, and something else — the wild hao plant that was to be her greatest discovery. "The deer make a you-you sound as they eat the wild hao plants."

Literature really is a remarkable thing.

THE IMPOSSIBLY YOUNG DOCTORS

IN THE 1980S, a TV scriptwriter thought of a funny idea. When you think of a family doctor at work, you probably think of a wise older person looking after children, right?

But what if the doctor WAS a child?

Some people liked his idea, but others said it couldn't happen. You have to go through years of school before you go to university, and you have to do a long course of medical study before you become a doctor. Most doctors start work at 25 or older.

So the scriptwriter wrote a story in which a child was found to be highly intelligent when he was still a toddler, and finished everything early — learning to read and write early, graduating from school early, going to university early, and so on.

The first episode of the show, called Doogie Howser, MD, was broadcast as a comedy show in the USA in 1989. (The letters MD indicate that a person is a Medical Doctor.)

It was very popular with the public in that country. But what they did not know was that the same things were happening in real life at roughly the same time.

A boy called Balamurali Ambati, who was in his early teens, was already at university in New York with the ambition of being a doctor.

And in 1990, when the show was entering its second year, another child was born in the USA who would also be described as a real-life Doogie Howser. His name was Sho Timothy Yano, son of a Japanese father and South Korean mother.

Looking back, we can see that both children followed similar lives to the fictional character. They started reading and writing when they were just toddlers, and went through school at a superfast rate, with their parents doing much of the teaching.

Yano went to university at the age of nine, graduated at 12, and then joined a prestigious university. But he chose to do a PhD in molecular genetics and cell biology first, while he was a

STEP C

teenager, and then do a medical degree afterwards. This meant that he was 21 when he became a working doctor.

Balamurali Ambati went straight into medical school at the age of 14, and graduated as a doctor at the age of 17. He told people he was lucky he was unusually tall (about 6 ft, which is 1.83 m), so people thought he was much older than he was, and he didn't feel out of place.

In 1995, he was listed in the Guinness Book of World Records as the world's youngest doctor, fully qualified by the age of 17.

The lives of both these children teach us something important: these days, even the imaginings of creative screen-writers can become true stories, such are the capabilities of the human race.

THE MOTHERLESS CHILD WHO SOLVED HIS FATHER'S PROBLEM

WHEN A YOUNG MOTHER died of illness, people felt sorry for her three little children, Gilberte, Blaise and Jacqueline.

What would happen to them?

Fortunately, the three children were looked after by their father, a judge, and his servants.

The judge decided that his children were unusually clever. Probably most parents think that about their children, but the judge actually did something about it — he decided that he himself would be their teacher, and they would all be home-schooled by him.

Blaise, who had been just three years old when his mother died, soon showed that he was extremely good with science and mathematics.

By the time he was a teenager, Blaise Pascal was writing scientific papers, just like a university professor.

At the age of 16, he wrote a paper about something called the Mystic Hexagram, which was a mathematical problem that had puzzled experts for years.

But then the family's luck turned bad again.

His father lost his job as a judge, and the family became very poor.

The man of the house eventually got a job as a tax collector, so they had some income. Yet the work was really hard, and the former judge asked his son Blaise to help him sort through thousands and thousands of sheets of numbers scribbled on paper.

Now all this happened a long time ago, in the 1600s in France, long before there were computers or calculators. That meant it was a difficult job to be a tax collector. Every sum had to be added up using pencil and paper, and it was really important that not one number was wrong.

Blaise found the job just as tough as his father did.

But the child was creative. He realized that because numbers

1
1 1
1 2
1 3 3 1
1 4 6 4 1
1 10 10 5 1
1 6 15 20 15 6 1
STEP C.

were logical, he should be able to build a machine that could process them, using a system of levers. You probably know what an abacus is. The device he designed was a bit like a small, automatic abacus, inside a box.

So, at the age of 16, he started to work on a portable calculating machine. Of course, these were not electric ones like we have — electricity had not really been discovered then, not for general use, anyway.

By the time he was 18, he had created a mechanical calculator that could add and subtract, and which gave the right answer every time. The machine was called Pascal's calculator or the Pascaline — and he became famous.

A few of his original calculators still exist, and you can see them in museums in Paris and in Dresden, Germany.

But the next time you use your calculator to do mathematics at school, spare a thought for the motherless son who created the first calculator, to help the father he loved.

Blaise Pascal grew up to become a famous scientist, mathematician, and Christian philosopher.

He said lots of interesting things that people are still discussing today, such as this: "The supreme function of reason is to show man that some things are beyond reason."

THE GIRL TORN BETWEEN TWO CAREERS

TEENAGER RACHEL CARSON WAS PUZZLED.

Most young people have no idea what they want to do when they grow up — but she had the opposite problem.

There were TWO things she really wanted to do. And she couldn't choose between them.

Rachel was born in 1907 on a farm in the United States and absolutely loved nature. So it seemed like she was destined to be a scientist.

But she loved reading novels, and her short stories had been published in a magazine. So it seemed like she was destined to be a writer.

Which was it to be? Scientist? Or writer? Rachel, who was a Christian, wrestled with the problem. Why had God given her such a challenge?

She was still confused when she applied to college. Rachel enrolled as an English student, so that she could study literature, and then decided she had made a mistake. She switched courses, starting again as a science student.

It was frustrating.

But she didn't have time to worry about this puzzle. Her family was very poor, and several members were suddenly struck by illness.

So that meant that after she finished college, she had to take whatever jobs she could find, to earn money to feed her troubled family.

Her life was quite difficult for a long time. But finally, after years of struggling, everything started to click into place.

Science is important, but very hard to explain — and the special skill of good writers is that they are great at explaining things. THAT was where she would fit in.

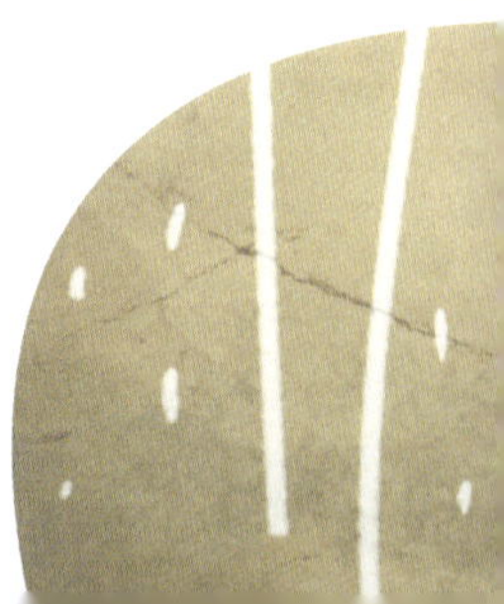

She realized that when she had switched from studying writing to studying science, all she was really doing was giving herself, a writer at heart, something important to write about.

Rachel also realized that the books she had read when she was young were great stories — but all had a nature theme. As a little girl, she loved Peter Rabbit, and as she became a teenager, she had read Moby-Dick, the story of a man trying to find a great whale.

Well, you may be able to guess the next part of Rachel Carson's story. Yes, she became a science writer. And in 1962, when she was 54 years old, she wrote a book called "Silent Spring", and that made her famous. It was a book about the harm that pesticides were doing to the environment. She died in 1964.

But that wasn't the end of the story. Her message inspired the setting up of the US Environmental Agency.

Today, most people know that humans are damaging the environment, and historians list Rachel Carson as one of the founders of the green movement.

KEEP READING

READING ABOUT THE LIVES of scientists and other discoverers adds to our store of knowledge, but we hope also leads us towards something much greater, which is wisdom.

This book is part of a series, which we hope you'll enjoy reading, and will spur you on to do your own scientific research.

The creators of this book wish you success in your explorations.

THE YOUNG SCIENTISTS SERIES

Book 1: SECRETS IN THE ROCKS
Five Astounding Tales of People Solving Mysteries Beneath Our Feet

Book 2: FABULOUS PHYSICS
Five Amazing Stories of People Who Solved Nature's Puzzles

Book 3: MAGICAL MATHEMATICS
Five Astonishing Stories of People Who Did Miracles with Numbers

Book 4: BREAKERS OF BARRIERS
Five Stunning Stories of People Demolishing Walls to Make History

Book 5: SCIENTIFIC PIONEERS
Five Incredible Tales of People Who Helped Develop the Scientific Method

Book 6: THE AMAZING QUANTUM
Five Awesome Stories of People Who Made a Revolution in Physics

Book 7: THE SCIENCE OF HUMANITY
Five Fascinating Stories of People Who Helped Us Understand Ourselves

Book 8: WOMEN OF DISCOVERY
Five Super Stories of Fabulous Females Who Made Scientific History

Book 9: THE INVENTOR'S SPARK
Five Marvelous Stories of People Who Helped Shape the Modern World

Book 10: ADVANCES IN ALCHEMY
Five Startling Stories of Chemistry and Biology

Book 11: THE CALL OF THE STARS
Five Wonderful Stories of People Looking to the Heavens

Book 12: MYSTERIES OF NATURE'S LAWS
Five Striking Stories of People Investigating the Deepest Puzzles of Reality

Published by

WS Education, an imprint of
World Scientific Publishing Co. Pte. Ltd.
5 Toh Tuck Link, Singapore 596224
USA office: 27 Warren Street, Suite 401-402, Hackensack, NJ 07601
UK office: 57 Shelton Street, Covent Garden, London WC2H 9HE

National Library Board, Singapore Cataloguing in Publication Data
Name(s): Vittachi, Nury, 1958– | Cheung, Step, illustrator.
Title: Breakers of barriers : five stunning stories of people demolishing walls to make history / author, Nury Vittachi ; illustrator, Step Cheung.
Other title(s): Young scientists series ; 4.
Description: Singapore : World Scientific Publishing Co Pte Ltd, 2017.
Identifier(s): OCN 969703107 | ISBN 978-981-3221-44-4 (paperback)
Subject(s): LCSH: Scientists--Juvenile literature. | Science--Juvenile literature.
Classification: DDC 509.22--dc23

British Library Cataloguing-in-Publication Data
A catalogue record for this book is available from the British Library.

All royalties received will be channelled to the National Book Development Council of Singapore (NBDCS) as a gift from the author.

First published 2017
Reprinted 2018

Printed in Singapore